ADRIFT

ADRIFT

A Collection of Poems

by Kristy Peloquin

Table of Contents

FLY

For Ryan

FRAY

Convalesce

The last time I prayed to God I lay dying in a mess of crisp white sheets. Days slid by and collided with one another in some back corner of my mind where things go to wait for me to remember them, like detritus hanging in trees after a flood. And everything ached. Sunlight, needles, a scar on my knee from when I was five. The prayer ached. I cobbled together some words in a line and pushed them out of my mouth. They resisted the way poems resist, clinging to my lips like trapeze artists. The prayer, what was it? Some request for life or death. A quiet apology for being. Pre-recorded vestiges I only had to recite. I remembered a shrine I saw in a mid-city parking lot. Plastic flowers stood resolute in their pink, yellow, red vivaciousness as rain poured down. A picture of the Virgin Mary had been taped to the concrete base of a light pole and there were beads, strings of beads that people pray with, strewn about. How did those beads work? What was their magic? I coughed and the prayer finally escaped. I watched it flutter around the room and throw itself against a window pane and then it was gone. The air conditioning kicked on. The sheets laid against me like a child. My body chattered on and on about injury.

Identity

I counted up the times I almost didn't make it home, a shivering list of moments, some languid and sprawling, others icy and specific. A quiet little parade of people went around inside of me, different people at different times, knowing different things. Some knew about twigs, creeks, and black soil fields. Others knew about tarpaper shacks and bad marriages, illness and motherhood, tributaries and sunlight. Little words to Jesus flitted about like stirred-up dust over all of them and I began to wonder at scars and memories and the shapes of my bones and the moraine deposits of long ago glaciers that carved me from the bedrock.

Locks

There's a scrambling in daylight, a scurrying into dark copses and leafy underbellies of plants, bodies pressed into shadowed doorways, tucked into rooms with shades drawn, splintered views for pinned-in pieces of ourselves we'd prefer not to have collected into mason jars and held aloft

even if there are holes in the lid. The curio cabinet grows cluttered with dust and fossils, shed snake skin and dried dragonfly wings, delicate as a whisper. Photographs curled and yellowing with age mark a time, a summer, when spindly-legged and new, I stood with the sun on my shoulders, my feet holding down the lawn where play spooled the hours into locks.

Now the photographs stand among the curious objects, the curious objects stand among the glass walls, and I mark them – this is when I was never shy,

this was before and before and before.

Clean

All best prescriptions for joy move through her like a song, one lyric married to another until sunlight cracks its way into dark old rooms made of dust. The house of her soul is derelict. Against the horizon, it is a tall bricks and sticks stalwart, something seen of many plains-going storms, the sort that scrape the land clean season after season. Feet in the dirt, she can remember rain on glass and after, the clean breath that cut away everything but the foundation.

Protected

We close the door so we can fight. We yell in a whisper because in the next room, our children grow. We wouldn't want to damage them, precious bright porcelain, soft velvet, sweet summer peaches. We worked so hard to craft this pretty life of rooms filled with matching curtains, rugs, bedspreads, warm hum of a refrigerator with always enough to eat, and it teeters on our shoulders, set against our necks like blocks of melting ice. Behind the door, cinched up in the walls, we are clumsy, we trip and tumble in the froth and tie accusations on one another, shove one another into corners, fall on each other. The space between us ignites, chases all the animals from the forest. But it's okay. We're quiet about it. We keep our children safe from ourselves.

Angel

In this tarpaper shack out on the edge of everything, I inspect the glut of my days for a memory I know is in there somewhere, a shimmering singing pinch of a day that still wrestles me into joy. Loose of my moorings, I rummage around in an old current, some old wreck of an ocean, for any sign of recognition. Had I come this way before? Did the fidgety waves remember me? Lapping at my edges, they say I was a catawampus malcontent in my younger days, and they do not know what I did with my shiny memory coin. They say, "You were bent at all corners like a junk yard license plate. We tried to help. We tried to make you new again." The moon, swinging in his sky swing of lavender stars, laughed a full belly laugh that shook me through to my rivets and sticks. "All they did was teach you about rust," he said. "The angel tried to help."

I remembered her then, that long-legged, wobbly angel whose eyes were too big for her face, heavy above her cheeks like stones sliding down a mountainside. When she blinked, little tufts of air fell on my arms. She climbed down out of the top bunk of space and slid into the bottom bunk with me. We put stickers of foxes and rabbits on the bottom of heaven, and after a while she said she was supposed to help me fit into the picture frame I was born with.

That picture frame – I'd carted it with me for years, placed it, empty, by every bed I'd ever slept in, dusted it, held it, pressed my lips against it, thinking someday

I would get in there, someday I would fit. The angel pushed and pulled and squeezed and pinched, trying to help me into the frame. She prayed and danced and asked God for some scissors. I stopped her there. I showed her some cactus needles in my palm and pencil lead that had been stuck in my calf since sixth grade. They were reasons. She frowned. "You're never gonna fit without the scissors," she said. It was a bright true fact spinning on its axis between us.

Inculcate

I would surrender if I could, but he's here with his words on tight and his eyes at my neck, ready to tell me what for and how it's gonna be. He can't remember where he came from or how we got here, but he knows he hates me. And he knows he pities me, too, or he should because Jesus and love, but he brushes off those mosquitos. He needs to focus. "Get it right," he tells himself. Sweat droplets teeter and shiver on his brow like little children in a pew. A sad, I-meant-to-do-this, this-is-exactly-how-I-planned-it glimmer flashes in his eyes. He presses the cold O mouth of a gun barrel under my chin. "Youuuu..." he manages through clinched teeth, shredding the word to pieces. What's left of it falls against my skin, warm and soft as kitten fur. I close my eyes, ready to hurt. Around us, a rain begins. Bits of tears, glass that twinkles, pages of books, strands of dna, tufts of pollen, memories of wind, and constellations fall headlong toward the ground all around us, trapping us together in this one moment that becomes our history.

Trauma

And then there's the morning you feel like you're missing something. The beat is there but the breath swings shallow in the eaves, waiting for the next emergency. You check things – phone, fingers, rim of your coffee cup, but all is in order. The eyes observe the infallible rules of things. All things obey, conform. Only the mind, inhabited by some wild force, bucks at the notion this is real. This body sitting, drinking, heaving thin cups of air at the room claims no one is home within the shell. No marionette attends the strings. But a long ago, far away version of self peers from a doorway flooded in light.

Womb

Slip into the marshlands, the mud water haven of reeds and long legged birds, round sinewed spectacles of grace and wings such that could cover me head to toe were I lucky enough. Instead, brackish bathwater cluttered with shampoo bottles, the distant call of the air conditioner as it hums pretend cool breezes into my face, and I sink down into the clutch coil of pent-up currents. Body of my body, bones of my bones, here we are again in an oval cup in the universe, stamped out womb of industry, predictable baptisms that require nothing in return. This is as close as I can get to faith and cleanliness, and for that someone will call me shallow.

Duende

It's maddening to be a fat clock ticking, talking with
my mouth crammed full of chicken feathers

as if chicken feathers were thoughts the way
butterflies are wings. I swear, this one bulb shack out
on the edge of everything is a monument to my soul,
old paper peeling and showing

a robin's egg blue gush of memory underneath,
improper and singing a whistle like a firework just let
loose of its moorings. I render down into black soils, at
the last of fingers – darkness

all around the nails as if scratching at fence posts or
gardens or wickedness.

See Through

It was me, caught in an open window, catching light,
throwing night, a closed window caught

in a storm. Whose window, windows, doors, walls,
houses, streets? Don't know,

doesn't matter. Lost

on a street near a row of boarded up houses, closed
windows that can't catch, won't catch,

couldn't catch my reflection even if they wanted to or
needed to, had the impulse,

knee-jerk reaction to – wouldn't.

Lost and going blind on this street, between these
houses made of walls, doors and what else? Windows.

If not windows, then

what am I made of? What is the world made of

and so on.

Match

I toss my hat into the ring to see what all bruises I can get to lay on me, swinging lights, fussy roar of an audience, every inside thing smashing through my skin to send me sailing forward. My fists sling through the air like water balloons, my elephant feet stumble, throw me over before I can land a single fat fist. My face slams the floor and the taste of the blood in my mouth says to me of memories, small ones, from I swear – a million years ago and I hear a song, something like waves at the ocean, something raspy and splintered, and made of hilarity. It holds me there,

right down on my knees.

Bones

This guy, I don't know his name, I don't recognize his face, drives us. We're heading down the interstate, the part of it that runs over the river and slides into downtown like a needle. One of us knows him, the driver. My friend, I think, knows him, that's why he's in the front seat while I'm in the back. I'm in the backseat, touching a hole in the vinyl seat covering, uprooting the orange foam underneath, rolling it between my thumb and forefinger till I'm bored of it and need more. We're driving. I worry, but they don't. I can't stop seeing us from the outside. I'm outside the car, wind-whipped, looking back in at all of us gunning down the highway. Through the window, I see the driver's face. I don't know him. I see my friend laughing next to him. My friend's teeth make me think of his bones. He has bones and so do I and all of our bones hurtle down the road. I'm in the backseat, as I've said. And this guy drives us. I think we're getting pretty good at dying. At least, it seems so.

Break In

And then there was the time the cops showed up at our door, 2 am, looking for Celestino, unfurling a warrant like a ramrod, commanding us to put our clothes on while they pushed into our shoebox in the sky, invading every corner of our pathetic little lives, dirty underwear on the floor, the cat box unscooped, empty bottles of wine like sentinels of our abuses. We didn't know Celestino. His face stared out from an old booking photo. Brown eyes, dark hair, just like me. Where had he gone, what had we done, the cops wanted to know. Our cat hissed at them. My lover tried to make peace. Celestino, just some guy with a drug history and us saying, "we don't know him, we don't know him" like we were swimming in waves so much bigger than ourselves, our voices lost in the walls, my arms crossed over my chest.

Educated

I'm turning inside out so often I can't remember which way is the way I ought to go. I leave post-it notes on lamp tables and windows, telling myself this is a real lamp table, this is a real window, but I'm not sure. A memory pastes itself to the walls, rolling glue over itself in long dripping strokes, strips of paper and glue coalesce like a reflection in a pond. I can see a time in a kitchen in a house years ago now when our voices ran the rough gauntlets, scraping us hard against rocks, depositing us soft against shores. My cheek on the wet sand. Your eyes carried downstream. The memory peels from the wall under its own wet weight, the heavy hulking glue, and underneath – glass.

Hunger

We're hungry now, washed up and carved out after saying to ourselves, It's fine. It'll be fine now. We wait at a table in an afterhours diner, inspecting our hospital bracelets for the truth of our names, the day we were born, our drug allergies. These are things we can say about ourselves with some degree of certainty. Other things are questionable. Like are we alive. What will tomorrow bring. The carnival of pancakes, butter pats, sticky syrup vessels, knives and forks, napkins, chitter chatter, plastic tablecloths belies the aches and swimming thoughts, but for now, it's fine. What color had love been. Would it be too much to ask for more.

Fire

We held hands in moonlight next to a large apartment building in which I had a room the size of a ring box. He had lovely dark hair in waves and eyes that clung to everything and a jaw, angular and full of stories. When he held me, it was like leaning into a window. He was all frame and visions, arms encircling me but missing me, a rabbit from a snare darting back into brambles. Outside of the apartment building, on the cement sidewalk speckled in glint, we waited for the firetrucks. The sirens howled to each other in the streets. He was responsible he said, for so many things he could not tell me. His hand slid into mine, long fingers over my knuckles. It'll be different now, he said.

Adrift

Christmas morning, kitchen floor, near the rusting metal legs of our dining table I said, I'll never leave you, which was, we knew, a lie. I'd been born broken and flighty, held in place by only the thinnest of threads, and I could fight myself down only sometimes. Most times, I choked. Many times, I died. Once, under a pre-dawn sky, I packed my clothes, my daughter, some food into our car and then we were gone, tumbled out of the nest and flying down backroads toward an ever-moving horizon. I cried thinking of him in the empty house with the gray shadows and the long, ringing silence of abandonment milling about in all the rooms. But I couldn't go back, not to him, not to that life, or the life before it, or the one before that. I'd made my escape. I thought, all will grow quiet in the bed of my body now. Dust will settle over the wounds. Everything will be fine.

FUME

Post-Colonial

I'm in here and all of it is out there. It pushes against the windows, wanting in, and I put my forehead to the glass, wanting out. It tells me stories of things that have happened, the homeless camp that was forced to move, the woman in the woods who was beaten, the days in needles spent. I counter with the palms of my hands where there is nothing but need. The sky is blue that ravages us. The sunlight casts its arrows until we can think of little else. A mouse tunnels into the powder fine drywall, scratches his way into the insulation, lines his nest with bits of plastic and shorn blanket threads, and stray strands of my hair. Here I am with my worry baked into fine tea biscuits.

We say to one another, Oh that was years ago now, as if the ashes weren't still floating around us, marking the currents of our breaths. We move along streets, duck into doorways, shuffle through rooms ablaze with conversation plumes, and we drift among the tufts of fine fallen new snow like we aren't cold, like we don't remember whatever heat whipped us into ruin.

Interrogation

You're in the other room and your language sounds like bouncy balls, dropping over and over, over and over. The cadence has at me – a bird fluttering in my face, frantic collision of feathers and eye lashes, and I can't breathe for fear of inhaling it all – the bird, the feathers, your voice.

When I was at the ocean last, I sat out on the edge of a sandbar far from shore. The tide was out and the sun shattered across the waves, sounding like wind breaking to pieces in a wind chime. I dug my fingers into the sand, feeling the sand as a living thing that gasped and had a heartbeat and ran away, grain by grain, in the waves. Down into the suck and softness, I clawed, my fingers digging, unearthing. I found a family of sand dollars and hoisted them to the surface, still alive, a thousand little arms writhing as I held them in my palm, in the crackling light. They smelled of salt and mud. I'd never seen them alive, only dead in souvenir shops. Their arms looked as though they were waving, but I knew they were throwing fists and prayers into the air, threatening, beseeching to be returned to the safety of the darkness, that warm bed of sand blankets.

What are you saying in that other room, under the hum of florescent lights? There your voice falls again. You pick it up and it falls against the walls like water, sloshing around us all.

Election Results

All the things I don't want to be true are in a day true,
glass globe true, a flustered and flailing against walls
until bloodied true. The dribble, the faucet leaky in a
back room where none of us wanted to go has flood-
bloomed. We thought we had forward moved, past
colors and greed and things cruel, but currents brew
in the back room, that place we never wanted to know
true, panting stink breath on our skin moves,
something solipsistic at our ears croons, moans,
chokes us blue and in this drowning I find you, foul-
hooked on a bright lure.

Vernacular

The hobbled feet go, casualties of a vague war, a profuse disturbance of who can say what and when and how, and where are we to go in all of that? A voice here for tea tables, a voice there for front lines. One is a lazy summer vacation abroad, where ideas are plucked from romantic old alleys and sweeping vistas of calm, the other plays board games with a cop at an inner-city apartment building so it won't sing in the streets with sirens. Where do we shove these precious little language packets, these tinctured forays, these cough syrup Cristal rosé ineptitudes and half-baked, still soft ideas? This one has a right to be heard, that one hasn't worked hard enough.

Race

Hustled up to the starting gate, we glance at one another like, what the hell are we doing here? Our nostrils flare, our muscular haunches are prone to run, but we don't know why. We did what they said. We hustled ourselves around all the right bends, learned all the right commands, let them onto our backs and tried so hard to be good. We snorted and whinnied. We wove our glorious intelligences into dust we could throw on top of serious questions and smother them – just like we'd been taught. Weave just this way, the answers to all, and so our hooves rake the dusty lanes, a crowd grinds to life in the stands, and we run.

Library

There were times we closed up our mouths, set the teeth against one another, stacks of bricks for the warding off of saying too much. We kept everything – our despondent dreaming, our deep knowing put away in the library of our malcontents, stitched shut into volumes as if we were afraid of them. Sometimes we still visit, wander the long aisles, sing a songbird's question into each dust filled corner, and the answers scream back at us from their taciturn covers.

Looking Glass

It's a risk we take to encounter our anger, to stare into its recalcitrant face. Maybe it has at us and we are gobbled up. Maybe we fall into its arms and weep like children against its ruddy coals. Maybe we hear the meditation it has been praying for us. Even as we are told that anger isn't a deep well, it whispers look, look, look and see.

Certainty

He says with certainty that he isn't one of us. We've seen him at the feed trough, his ugly old need to consume mirroring ours. We've heard him snarl, felt him push us out of the way so he can pack his paunch, and we let him because we know what hunger is like, but then, we've seen how, in the dark when we're all supposed to be sleeping, keeping each other warm and safe, he stands upright on his legs and screeches to the world that we are disgusting beasts who have eaten all his food and taken all his space, and really, we should be loaded up and taken away.

Rundberg ICE Raid

I'm in the same line as you at the grocery store. Like you, this is where I buy my bananas, chicken breasts, Band-aids, toilet paper, cat food. This is where I grip the grocery cart and hope that the person who used it before me didn't have the stomach flu. This is where I worry what I forgot and should I get a loaf of bread or do I already have one at home and what's all this going to cost. I'm here in the same line as you, plopping my treasures and burdens on the conveyor belt like they are going to be smelted into something beautiful. You place the divider between your things and my things. You don't talk to me or look at me when you do it, but we're together – listening to the rustle of items being bagged, to the pulsing, repetitive hum of "How are you today? Did you find everything you need?" and to the insistent bleep bleep bleep. In here, we're all moving to the same tune. We all know the steps and how to move our arms and how to avoid one another's eyes. We're all here trying to get done, to get home to our little nests in the walls, to our people we love, to our papers and books and screens and windows and toilets and sinks and dishes and carpets and ceilings and doors we don't have to open, and closets we can hide in, and backyards we can run through should the need arise.

Disappointments

How can we leave when we're trapped? Even as we're shooed with brooms and barks and our feet dance on landmines, every which way – walls. And down those walls run voices. A thick grease mess of tar and scoldings. Shame on us for leaving. Shame running all over us until we slip, tumble, bruise like grapes. This isn't the artful scurrying the voices are after, the perfect tenuous fear. This is the giggly belly of the whale, sloshing with inconsistencies. How ugly our tiny mouse feet are! What trouble they cause.

Detained

When you're locked up, you try not to ask too many questions. There is a premium on them. The space they take up in your mouth. The itty-bittiest time you have to ask them. So you sew them together in a long blanket, a stitch here for "when can I see my family" and a stitch there for "how much is this going to hurt?" And there are days when the blanket stretches to the sun. Or it runs home to your house and knocks on the door. Your lover's eyes – soft worry nests. If you could, you would burn the blanket like incense on an altar. Or pull each thread to see how many prayers cling to it. Or maybe you would lie down on the petal ground, and let the threads hold vigil over you.

Satellite

It never occurred to the boy with the bright mind that out there – in the pharmacological blue sky, they thought he was a fallen, fat-mouthed monument, a burnt out satellite, once full of promise and orbits, now fizzling in a field someplace, quite dissatisfying. He had made a house on the edges of some old books, the floor a pod of humpbacked spines, the windows made of holes burrowed by thoughts with wings. He collected his ideas in aquariums, tended them, fed them, gave them a treasure chest whose lid opened with bubbles and then closed again and the ideas multiplied, teemed at the ready with some kind of magic. But they said he wasn't right. Something too loose jointed in that one. We only like things that are the same as us. The same as us is best, trust us.

Legitimate

This is something, I suppose, holding my little piece of paper that legitimizes my window frame soul. All that pouring in of views and sounds of birds chirping or chipping or chiming away like hollow metal tubes full of tinkling sunlight. This paper grows limp in the humidity. I am because this is, and now I have a face and a name and I walk around like a real soul. I get to be – brown and baked in the sun like pottery, all mud and clay, all memories and ash, all children and mothers and fathers and lovers and caked moonlight. The paper says the day I was born – one day, one birth, one time among many that I opened my eyes.

Veteran

I heard a man tell another man that "blood didn't bother him" and that he could be a paramedic easy because "he didn't have any emotional reaction to seeing bodies in bits." Our eyes crashed together over the dull gray linoleum, pocked walls, fluorescent lighting wheezing in its tin housing. He sat tall in his seat even when slouching, too long for a normal chair, but he had his manners, yes ma'am, no ma'am, and affinities for things like trucks and motorcycles and drink.

In January, he'd gotten a DWI for sleeping in his truck in a Walmart parking lot after a night at a local bar. "The bitch of it was, I wasn't even driving!" he said, raising his hands in the air like he was waiting for something to fall into them. Then he leaned back and tapped the toe of one of his boots. "Wasn't always this way," he said.

He told me how he'd been on active duty, checking IDs at a road station. A car full of five people blew right past them, past signs and men yelling at them to stop. A warning shot rang through the air, but the car kept going. "So I unloaded my .50 cal into their vehicle. Killed 'em all." He paused, lifted the cap off of his head, scratched his hairline and put the cap back on. "Then command said I had to go search the bodies for guns and weapons, so I had to go to the car and rummage around in the blood and body parts. After that, nothing, no feelings. Well, that and the pigs. They brought in these pigs so we could practice controlling femoral artery bleeds. We had to pack the wounds and well, you know... anyway, things don't bother me now. I can flip a switch in my mind. I don't feel things if I don't want."

American Dream

Quiet nature of night, whose eyes circle slowly on warm thermal currents, pours over my chalky bones the way water negotiates the stones of a river. All eyes on the shore now, the land of shame and desperation puffed up into scoops of walls and windows, topped with roofs to repel the sky, that chatter box, that know-nothing tedious hum of stars. My body, other bodies, pinned to clotheslines in backyards shiver in the night air, picked apart by moonlight sitting on a blade of grass. The wind chases our marrow from our bones and sends night whistling though us, vessels of catastrophe, delicate canvases of the universe.

Crossing

Stopped at a railroad crossing, the train slides along the rails, a blur, a broad stroke of paint

blue but mostly rust gushing behind two red blinking lights. He is ripped out of his seat, slung into the heat of slurring memory, heaviness sagging against wood paneled walls, a whale of a beast beached in a fake falsetto forest holds him by the neck, yelling again and again, did he know what had been done to her? The scream, the warning siren of the train hollering out of the tunnel before him, grinding metal on metal behind the lights. He thinks, I am the rails, the weight is upon me.

Brittle

The will you, won't you in silence is the will of you
leashed to a lamp pole, dark street, yellow mid-city
light going scattered in heat, even at night. The
sidewalk under your shoes cracks itself with tree roots
and runs out just when you need it, just when blues
become some kind of blood in you. Derelict beauty of
a you-town dream, clustered and flustered by you-
town fiends, runs and falls and skins a knee and in the
wound – diamonds.

FLY

Border Wall

You stood in your garden and I stood in mine. We traded leaves back and forth over a fence. You said you could see the whole world in the veins. When seasons came, we cuddled together against the fence and used our memories as blankets where I said, one time I lit a fire in the palm of my hand, which bled to my hair, and spilled into my eyes, and all at once I collapsed into ash. You said you kept a flashlight by your bed to keep monsters away, but the monsters only used it to blind you. This is how we love each other. Under great canopies of climbing suns we cling to each other's stories. I throw petals over the fence. You slide stones under it. I give you sticks that fell from my tree. You show me a caterpillar with green dots. I tell you about the river under the fence. You mention the threats you saw on tv. Through the dirt, we touch fingertips and make promises. Even as men come to separate us, we make promises. Even as the river is sucked dry and a hateful heat floods into the streets, we make promises.

Sticks

I keep asking, I keep asking, does it matter, does it matter, like a burr stuck in the heel of some child self, the self that falls into the grass, under a blue sky hollowed with laughter. The harness in my mouth is set, and I'm the fields, and I'm the toil. There the hobbling of two feet go, I'm in the springs with the leaves and things. At night in a cobweb, I'm strung up in a Christmas light nebula of memory and love. Love, the kind that has at me like a rash, bites and reddens my arms, my back, behind my knees and on my lips. I'm wrong and it's wrong and I tie all the little worries into ribbons into skies above deserts on the ends of said wrong sentences and bred wrong day dreams until feathers on a current go. Until erosion and sands freeze into stone.

Anchors

In her eyes was some kind of scary warning, some afterthought of the kind of wings she bore, the children tucked in the crux of her arms and the strength humming in the little lines of her hands. Everything she had been through, I couldn't know, but still we said our hellos like we were the same kinds of people, as if trying were something like the being. We nodded our heads – heavy-weight fighters, dead on our feet. We moved through our days inside a parade of things that needed doing, against a busy backdrop of work and bus rides and sick kids and bodies listing off new pains daily. There wasn't time for talking or space for things like friendship. But in the end, we knew that sitting in some back alley orangey light, our feet in a gutter, heads among power lines, we'd find each other and cast anchors around one another to keep from floating away.

Seeds

I'm dying with a great gush of paper clips flooding from my mouth and tape knotted in my hair and thoughts being born only to shrivel and die in the thin squealing florescent lights while the desk stares on. We know each other. I ask the desk to hide me, and it does. It forgets I have a name, a face. It's a game we play. It remembers when it had twigs and leaves; I try not to embarrass it by imagining. It shares its dust with me, and we sit covered, until spring, until outside the grass reappears and like pocketed mice, very tired of seeds, we awake in a mound of shells.

Stars

That blue sky carves out my chest the way love eats a
canyon into every solid argument,

and the dry pale grass says I'm a stupid ruiner of views.
Waste of space. Pitiful linear time monger, but the sky
has a longer memory. It remembers the time we set
sail, the stars sticking to us like brittle bits of shells,
and we glittered in the darkness, us coughing up
blood, all frail, all stacks of cells, fuming hungry needy
things with language and hearts like sponges and
enough dreams to keep the lights burning as long as
we need them.

Predisposed

You will know because it will be told to you over and over, a mantra skipping across open water, the wobbling a sign of its dedication. You will know and will learn that one path glows in the woods. One set of train tracks seethe among the trees. One river. One hand pointing. One voice fussing. You will think to try paths through thickets, summits, etched desert faces gaping at your audacity, even paths though graveyards on mesa tops, or pressed down into canyon bottoms

but you will see. You will know. One mantra. One brush stroke. One prick of a needle. One hewn handhold burning in the sun.

Storms

Pieces of rusted wire twisted together and holding onto fences in all kinds of weather. Come what may. Only itches when rain is near. Like I have wounds that the weather knows. As if my body converses with storms.

In the ash of yesterday, there is a mothering of the world I want to do, a gathering of the world into my arms, an embrace made of bedtime stories, soft light, comfortable blankets and crooning words which settle over us, leaves let go of a bough.

Soil

Anymore the ghosts standing in the fields are singing
some wisp of a rumination that purls

across the plow lines like memory folding upon itself,
looking into the lines of their hands,

they see - each thin tributary is illuminated with soil -
the storehouses our palms can be.

They move through tree lines on the far side of the
black swath, beyond is the lovely creek,

her eyes are always on the leaves and sky, and she's
holding the secrets of fish and springs

in her cool clear belly.

Roots

I rubbed my cheek against the rough crust of an old oak, ants running vertically between shards of bark thick with things buried and brooding in its skin. "How do you do it?" I wept into its craggy arms, my skin scratched and red-rashed from my troubles. "How do you stay still all your life?" The oak, a quiet summoner of winds, endured me like a mild fever. My questions flitted around me, landing on me, licking their legs, stroking their long antennae, tickling and annoying me, blessing me with bustle and color, before trailing off in all directions, taking their answers with them.

Base

There's a way we swing through trees like, this is this and that is that, and the sun melts all over the horizon day after day. Inside our small house with walls leaning on one another for support against the elements, we hold hands and wonder what will happen when the snow becomes too heavy, how many winters from now will that be? There's a crack in the foundation where sometimes I disappear. Down into the concrete cold conglomerate and into the soil damp with sadness. Up there in the house world, people don't remember. But down here in the soil, we cannot forget. Below the soil is the bedrock. Below the bedrock is the water. And down down down is the hot beating heart of us all – a wicked, warm loveliness that licks at our names and the tips of our ears, whispering.

Blood

I've been trying to find the trails which are hidden in the snow. The meadows, clean fire of white in the sun, stretch at all edges into trees. The trails run soft in darkness, wet with melt, secluded threads to some unknown end, and I desire them. At night when the hour is late and I wake up with thoughts crystalizing in the dim suggestions of my room, I want them, what is at the end of them, the rough perennial beauty of their grasp, to be dragged down into hollows, and lifted into light. I want these veins beating with wild blood to connect us all.

Colors

In paint-by-number, the light hits us here, there, in predictable fragments. Thin blue lines tell where our colors go, but they don't get us very far. What holds views during the day throws reflections at night. My face, a pond of fish and reeds, and your face bloodied at its bottom lip. I look for the teeth when you speak, delight to see the crooked one, the chipped one. I thirst, I mean thirst like a skipped beat, for knowing you, not the lines or the colors, but the scent of cedar, sound of your voice hung up on song or cool brush of some memory dancing across the floor between us for us both to know.

Ambient

We're all aching to find the path, toiling as we do, fingers searching the soil, digging the roots, shuffling the earthworms and grubs and bits of flint for that thing we're supposed to know, a glowing beneath the tundra of cities and cast off crusts of bread.

In the center of the dream, we shipwreck, clinging to bits of debris, broken idols, broken glass, whole coils of moonlight peeled from a memory. Waves lift our bodies to the stars, pull us back towards sand. We have a song which is our breathing. We forget what we were and become only stars sand salt – and waves. Even once land appears under our soft feet again, even when buildings yawn in our faces, we talk about currents, gentle storms waltzing in our eyes. It never was any different.

Idealized

If I go dreamy in a thimble, sailing on the open heart of this day – and maybe a jazz note or ten, and maybe the soft fuss of clouds or sheets, or a lover's little touch – would you write letters back to the mainland with me? We could forget bombs swirling out over the Atlantic basin or icebergs leaping to their deaths because of whispers they heard about warm waters to the south. We could eat the snacks I brought and listen to our heartbeats and give everything a name the way everything names us and calls us brittle glints of light and ignores us. Could we find something in the snaps of sparks twirling up from our campfire on an island far away, waves away, scoops of lemony sun and shivering stars away, that could save us? If we go dreamy, can we put the icebergs back?

Crumbs

I want to fall down into the belly of this poem with you. With our arms spread and backward falling, I want us sinking into the downy soft core of this poem. I want us nibbling at its crusty edge, discovering its burnt corner. I want our jaws stiff and painful from too much sweetness, our lips swollen from too much salt. In the belly of the poem, let's make a house of cinnamon sticks and toasted bread. Let's paint our walls with honey and stitch sprinkles into the ceiling almost like stars, almost like constellations of wish confetti, almost like a river with tiny bright ships sailing. The belly of this poem can hold us. Beyond the stiff throat tosses out Frisbees of phonemes, and below, the intestines sprawl in darkness, but here in the belly of this poem with our shimmery sugar crystal gardens, let's lie in the wheat with our fingers in the frosting.

Faith

A paper robot I was staying in a hotel with told me someone had abducted it and poked needles into its eyes. I tilted her face to the light and could clearly see needle holes in the paper of her eyes, but then hotel staff told me something completely different, that the robot had been causing trouble, tipping things over and being rude to people, and I didn't know who to believe.

I told the robot, look, I can't help you if you aren't honest with me. Then we had to run away because someone was after her, the same person who'd poked her eyes with needles, so we got in a limo and drove away to some strange town with houses, small and white with tiny green yards, and then squirrels stole the robot's magic.

I started chasing them to get the magic back. The magic was the end of a piece of silverware bent into a ring. As the squirrels made off with it, they jumped in a river. I jumped in after them and we were floating down the river, the squirrels in front of me with the silverware magic ring held over their little heads, until I finally got it from them and said, I really wish this could make me fly because I'm desperate to fly! And then a giant bird swooped down and got me.

About Atmosphere Press

Atmosphere Press is an independent full-service publisher for books in genres ranging from non-fiction to fiction to poetry, with a special emphasis on being an author-friendly approach to the challenges of getting a book into the world. Learn more about what we do at atmospherepress.com.

We encourage you to check out some of Atmosphere's latest releases, which are available at Amazon.com, BarnesandNoble.com, and via order from your local bookstore:

Ghost Sentence, poems by Mary Flanagan

That Scarlett Bacon, a picture book by Mark Johnson

That Beautiful Season, a novel by Sandra Fox Murphy

What I Cannot Abandon, poems by William Guest

Such a Nice Girl, a novel by Carol St. John

Makani and the Tiki Mikis, a picture book by Kosta Gregory

What Outlives Us, poems by Larry Levy

How Not to Sell, nonfiction by Rashad Daoudi

All the Dead Are Holy, poems by Larry Levy

Bello the Cello, a picture book by Dennis Mathew

Rescripting the Workplace, nonfiction by Pam Boyd

Surviving Mother, a novella by Gwen Head

Winter Park, a novel by Graham Guest

About the Poet

Kristy Peloquin is a poet, memoirist, teacher, and writing group leader in Austin, TX. She graduated from Texas State University with a BA in English, summa cum laude honors, in 2006, and went on to earn an MFA in poetry in 2009. She is a teacher at Austin Community College in Austin, Texas.